Awesome ALPHA MAZE

by Rolf Heimann

Troll

First published in the United States by Troll Communications L.L.C.

Text and illustrations copyright © 1991 Rolf Heimann

Printed in USA.

Design by Roland Harvey Studios

ISBN 0-8167-3698-7
10 9 8 7 6 5 4 3 2 1

Commander Xora wore a grave expression as she entered the meeting of the Ixenstein Intergalactory Exploration Society, in the company of the latest robot Alphalpho.

"Fellow aliens," she said, "I have bad, bad news. Captain Zopp has been captured while exploring the mysterious planet Earth, and he is now being held prisoner there in some zoo. I need two volunteers to go and find him."

"I'll go!" cried Vaxx.

"And I!" said Moxx.

"Count me in as well!" cried Xoxenackbobenbobbensteex.

Commander Xora smiled proudly. "Didn't I tell you, Alphalpho, that we can count on our men? Captain Zopp was a first-class explorer and we need him back. We always learned a lot from his missions, even his failed ones. Tell them, Alphalpho."

Alphalpho adjusted his volume control and explained, "We have already learned three important things from his trip to Earth. Firstly, never wear animal suits when on Earth. Secondly, always carry a spare can of Flixen fuel, because it is not yet available there. Frankly, I can't see how earthlings manage without it."

"And thirdly?" asked Vaxx, growing impatient.

"Yes, thirdly," continued Alphalpho, "it is necessary to train you explorers better before you go. You know, teach you some of the local languages and generally sharpen your wits and powers of observation. I have been programmed to help in these matters as I take you through our newly constructed, animated Alphamaze. It contains a maze that you must follow, and while you are doing that, you must recognize the letters of the alphabet and find a number of things beginning with each letter."

"How many things?" asked Moxx.

Moxx was beginning to get a bit worried. It all sounded rather difficult to him.

"All in all there are more than one thousand things to find," boasted Alphalpho.

"More than a thousand!" gasped the explorers in despair. "We'll never be able to find that many."

"Certainly not," stated Alphalpho proudly. "Only I am programmed to see them all."

Commander Xora explained, "If you find half of them you will qualify for our rescue mission. Are you ready to try our new Alphamaze, Vaxx and Moxx?"

"Yes, ma'am!" answered Vaxx and Moxx, snapping to attention.

"What about me?" asked Xoxenackbobenbobbensteex.

"Ah yes, about you..." said Commander Xora, scratching her antennae. "You see, it's nothing personal...it's just your, er, your name — it's sort of rather long. To tell the truth, Alphalpho isn't programmed to cope with names that are longer than ten letters."

"You could call me Xox for short," suggested Xoxenackbobenbobbensteex.

"That would help," admitted the Commander, "but we have a special secret mission for you. You see, we couldn't find many words that start with a Q, an X or with a Z, so I want you to pop down to these sections and hide a few shapes that look like these letters, just to give Vaxx and Moxx something extra to look for."

"Yes, ma'am!" cried Xoxenackbobenbobbensteex with enthusiasm. "Consider it done. Oh boy, I'll make it really hard for them."

"Good man," said the Commander, "I knew I could rely on you, Xoxenack..."

"Just call me Xox."

"Good man. Off you go and pull up your socks, Xox," said Commander Xora.

(That was typical of Commander Xora — she could never resist making little jokes like that.)

Beware the boa constrictor! And you can find more than a hundred other things beginning with either B or C.

6

11

There's Holmes the investigator, an instrument incorrectly held and dozens more H and I words.

17

19

23

"**I** am proud of you!" said Commander Xora as the two fearless explorers arrived at the end of the track. "How did they perform, Alphalpho?"

Alphalpho did not look very impressed.

"The mazes weren't so difficult," explained Vaxx, "but Alphalpho must be joking when he says there are more than a thousand things to find."

"I am not programmed to joke," interrupted Alphalpho. "I have a list of the words. Here it is. I admit it includes some pretty weird and difficult words..."

"Remember," added Commander Xora, "so far we have only introduced you to the English language. There are hundreds of different languages on Earth, and many ways to write them down. I guess that's why it is such an interesting place. After you have rescued Captain Zopp, Alphalpho will continue to train you. I promise that you will never run out of things to learn about Earth. We have programmed Alphalpho to teach you how to make pancakes, how to repair door locks, to say 'hello' in Swahili, and how to build a birdhouse using nothing but a Swiss army knife. But first of all, I want you to go through the maze one more time."

"Again?" cried Vaxx and Moxx in surprise.

"Yes. Tell them Alphalpho."

"You must find the things on the list that you were unable to find before," explained Alphalpho. "And keep your eyes peeled for anybody that looks like Captain Zopp. We have hired ten fellow aliens to pose as Zopp and hide somewhere. Off you go!"

The Answers...

A: abyss, accident, acorn, acrobats, agriculture, airplane, airport, akimbo, alien, alligator, alps, American flag, anchor, angel, angling, animal, antenna, antlers, ape, apex, apiarist, apple, apron, aqueduct, arch, Argentine flag, ark, arm, armada, armadillo, armor, arrow, artist, asp, astronaut, astronomer, atoll, Australian flag, Austrian flag, automobile, awning, axe.
B: baby, badger, baggage, balcony, ball, ballet, balloon, bananas, band, Band-Aid, bandages, bandana, barn, barrier, barrel, bars, basket, bat, bathe, bathtub, battery, battle, bay, beach, beak, beam, bear, beast of burden, beaver, bed, beehive, Belgian flag, bell, belt, bench, beret, bicycle, binoculars, bird, black, blimp, blind, blossom, blow, blue, board, boat, bolt, bomb, bones, bonnet, book, bottle, bound, bovines, bow, box, boxing gloves, boy, bread, bricks, bride, bridegroom, bridge, brook, broom, brush, bucket, buffers, bulb, bulldog, bull's-eyes, bunny, bus, butter, butterfly, buttons.
C: cactus, cake, caliber, camel, camp, can, Canadian flag, candle, canister, canoe, cannon, captain, car, caravan, cargo ship, carousel, carrot, cascade, (suit) case, castle, cat, catapult, catch, caterpillar, cathedral, cattails, cell, cellar, cello, cemetery, center, chain, chair, chalice, champagne, channel, chessboard, chicken, child, chin, chimney, choir, chorus, church, circus tent, climb, clock, clogs, close, closed, cloud, clown, coach, coast, coat, coat hanger, cobra, coffee, cogwheel, collision, comb, combat, concert, constrictor (boa), cook, corgi, corner, couch, couple, cow, crab, cradle, crane, creek, crisis, crocodile, crook, cross, crossbones, crow, crowd, crown, crutch, cucumber, culprit, cup, curtains, cushion, cutlery, cygnet.
D: dachsund, daffodil, dalmatian, damsel (in) distress, danger, Danish flag, dappled, daredevil, deer, delta, desert, destruction, devil, diamond, Diana, dice, dinghy, dingo, dinosaur, dirigible, diver, dodo, dog, doll, dominoes, donkey, door, dove, drag, dragon, dragonfly, dress, drip, ducks, dunce, dunes, dwarf, dynamite.
E: eagle, ear, echidna, egg, Eiffel Tower, electrician, elephant, eleven, elk, emporer, empty, emus, England, envelope, equation, eye.
F: face, factory fall, family, farm, father, faucet, feathers, fence, fender, fern tree, fiddle, field, find, finger, fire, firemen, firetruck, fish, five, flag, flamingos, flight, float, flock, flower, fly, foal, follow, food, foot, foreground, forest, fork, fortress, fountain, four, fowl, fox, frog, fruit, fry, full, funeral.

G: gallows, game, garden, gargoyle, gate, German flag, ghost, giant, giraffe, girl, give, glass bottle, gloomy, glove, goal, goat, golf, golf ball, golf club, gondola, goose, gorilla, grab, grandfather, grasp, grass, grave, green, grown, guitar, gull.

H: hair, half, hammock, hand, handle, harp, hat, hay, head, heart, hedge, hedgehog, help, herd, hexagonal harbor, high, high-tension, hill, hippopotamus, hockey stick, hoe, hog, hold, Holmes (Sherlock), home, honey, hook, horrible, horse, hospital bed, house, Hovercraft, hundred, hunt, hurry, hurt, hut, hydroplane.

I: ibis, ice blocks, ice cream, idiotic invention, igloo, ill, imp, Indian, indisposed, industry, inferno, ingredients, injection, ink, insect, instrument — incorrectly held!, inundated, investigator, Irish flag, island, Italian flag.

J: jacket, jaguar, jam, Japanese flag, jar, javelin, jazz, jealous, jelly, jester with jingle bells, jetty, jolly, Jonah, jonquils, journal, judge, juice, jumbo jet, jump, jumper, jumping Jack, jungle.

K: kangaroo, keel, keen, ketch, kernel, key, kilometer, king, kiosk, kiss, kiwi, kiwi fruit, Kleenex, knee, knife, knight, koala.

L: ladder, lagoon, lamb, lamp, land, lap, last, laugh, lava, lawn mower, leaf, leak, leap, leash, leave, leeks, left, leg, lemon, leopard, letter, level, lift, light, lighthouse, lightning, lilac, lilies, limit, line, lion, lips, lit, little, lizard, llama, load, lobster, lock, locomotive, log cabin, lollipop, long, look, lots, lovers, low, luggage, lute.

M: macaroni, mace, magpie, mail, many, map, maple leaf, march, marines, marionettes, market, masks, massive, mattress, maze, medal, medic, melon, mermaid, men, mess, Mexican, microphone, milestone, milk, mill, mine, minstrel, mirror, missile, monk, monkey, monument, moon, mortar, motel, mother, mountain, mouse, moustache, mouth, movie, musician, muzzle.

N: nail, Navy, neck, neon sign, Neptune, nest, net, new (growth on tree stump), newspaper, newt, nine, Noah, noodles, noon (on clock), Norwegian flag, nose, nostrils, nugget, number, nun, nurse, nut, nutcracker.

O: oasis, obelisk, obese, oblique, observatory, observer, ocean, octave, octopus, okapi, old, Olympic rings, omnibus, one, onion dome, onlooker, orangutan, oranges, orchestra, orchid, ostrich, outboard motor, outrigger, oval, oven, overjoyed, overalls, owl.

P: package, paddle, paddle wheel, page, pagoda, paintbrush, painting, pair, palette, palm tree, pan, panda, panic, pants, (Sancho) Panza, paper, parachute, park, parrot, pavilion, peach, peacock, pear, pedal, pelican, pen, pencil, pendulum, penguin, pentagon, people, persons, petal, photographer, piano, picnic, picture, pie, pier, pillow, pineapple, pink, pipe, pirate, pizza, plaid, plane, plate, platform, play, pleased, plenty, plight, pneumatic tire, pocket, pointed, pointing, polar bear, police, polka dot, pollution, poodle, poor, port, portrait, post, postman, pot, potato, priest, prison, profile, propeller, pupil, puppy, pursue, pussycat, pyramid, python.

Q: quarrel, quarry, quarter, quartet, quadruped, queen, question mark, quick, (Don) Quixote, quotation mark.

R: rabbit, race, racquet, radio, radishes, railway, rainbow, rat, raven, razor blade, rear, red, regatta, repair, revolutionary, rhinoceros, rickshaw, ridiculous, ring on Saturn, rings (on tree stump), rivets, road, robust, robot, rock, rocket, roll (of paper), rook (on chessboard), rope, rose, rough, royal, rudder, rug, ruin.

S: saber, sack, sad, safety pin, sail, sailor, salt, sand, sandal, Santa Claus, sarcophagus, Saturn, sausages, scared, scarf, scooter, scorpion, screw, scythe, sea, sea horse, seal, seat, see, seven, skier, skis, shadow, shamrock, shark, sheep, shell, sheriff, shine, ship, shoe, shopping cart, short, shrimp, shutters, signal, silhouette, silly, sink, six, skeleton, sleigh, slow, small, smile, smoke, snail, snowmen, soap, soccer ball, sole, south, Southern Cross, spacecraft, spear, sphinx, spider, spiderweb, spiral, spoon, spring, spurs, squirrel, stamp, stand, star, steam, steering wheel, steps, stern, stick, stone, strap, stretcher, string, stripes, stubble, sugar, sun, sunglasses, suspended, swine, sword, symbol, synagogue.

T: table, tail, tall, tambourine, tandem (bike), tango dancers, tank, tap, tarantula, target, tart, taxi, tea, tear, teddy bear, telephone, telescope, television, temple, tempest, ten, tent, terminal, thief, thousand, three, throat, thunderstorm, tie, tiger, timber, tire, toad, toilet, tomato, tongue on tiki, top, torch, toss, tortoise, tourists, tow, towel, tower, tractor, traffic, tram, transportation, traveler, tree, triangle, tricolor, tricycle, trip, tripod, Trojan horse, trombone, trousers, truck, trumpet, trunk, tub, tugboats, tulips, tumble, tunnel, turban, turtle, turtledove, typewriter.

U: ukulele, umbrella, underground, underwear, undressed, unicorn, unicycle, uniform, United States' flag, United Kingdom's flag, unsinkable, unusual, urn.

V: vacuum cleaner, valley, vampire, van, vase, vegetables, veil, ventriloquist, victim, victor, view, village, villain, vine, violet, violin, viper, volcano, volleyball, volume, vulture.

W: wagons, waist, waiter, walkie-talkie, wall, wallaby, wand, wanderer, warship, wart, washing, wasp, watch, water, waterfall, wattle, wave, wax candle, way, whale, wharf, wheel, whiskers, white, windows, windsurfing, wine, wing, winner, wipe, witch, wolf, woman, wombat, wood, wool, work, wrist, wrong.

X: Xmas tree, X-rays, xylophone.

Y: yacht, yak, yank, Yankee, yardarm, yarn (on rope), yashmak, yawl, year (on calendar), yell, yellow, yelp, yo-yo, yodel, yogi, yoke, yolk, young, yucca tree, yule log.

Z: zebra, (New) Zealanders, zeppelin, zigzag, zipper, zoo.

Note: Words beginning with either letter can be found throughout each double-page opening. For instance, B-words can be found on the C-side, and C-words can be found on the B-side. And by the way, the ten fellow aliens posing as Captain Zopp are on pages 5, 7, 11, 13, 15, 18, 23, 25, 29 and 30.